THE FACE OF LOUISIANA

THE FACE
OF
LOUISIANA

Photographs by
ELEMORE MORGAN

Text by Charles East

LOUISIANA STATE UNIVERSITY PRESS
BATON ROUGE

Copyright © 1969 by
Louisiana State University Press

Manufactured in the United States of America
by Steck-Warlick Company, Austin, Texas
Library of Congress Catalog Card Number 78–86493
SBN Number 8071–0913–4

INTRODUCTION

What a pity it is that Elemore Morgan did not live to write his own introduction. Then he could have told us what Louisiana meant to him, though even that would have been a second-best thing: it is in the photographs that we see his vision. And so the greater pity is that he did not live to select, or to direct the selection of, the photographs which comprise this book. One thing we can be sure of: they would not be precisely the same photographs that his son and I, after going through the many thousands of his prints, have included.

Had we elected to bring together *The Best of Elemore Morgan,* or *The Art of Elemore Morgan,* the job would have perhaps been easier. But from the beginning we conceived of the book as something larger than that—not merely a collection of one man's work but a record of his time and place: Louisiana over the span of twenty years, more or less, in the middle years of the twentieth century. Or, to put it another way, the last twenty years in the lifetime of the photographer.

Elemore Morgan died one Sunday afternoon in the spring of 1966. Later that year Elemore Morgan, Jr., and I sat down in his father's darkroom-office for what was to be the first of many such sessions. Was there a book here? As we sorted through that amazing collection of prints and proof-prints and negatives, the answer came: a clear affirmative. But there were, we discovered, obstacles. For one thing, Elemore had never set out deliberately to catch the composite image of his state, only some of the separate parts of it. He had collaborated with novelist Frances Parkinson Keyes on a book called *All This Is Louisiana,* but that was early in his career as a photographer. Later, as his assignments grew, he built upon that coverage. Together with writer Ed Kerr he roamed the state taking pictures to illustrate Ed's stories for the Louisiana Forestry Association magazine *Forests & People.* Many of Elemore's best photographs were taken during this period, and in 1962 he brought one hundred of them into a book called *The Lower Mississippi Valley.*

At the time of his death he was in the midst of work on two other projects. One was a series of photographs to illustrate *The Living Geology of Louisiana*. The other—and it was perhaps the most ambitious thing he had up to then attempted, and certainly the most unusual—was a photographic essay on a single tree, an ancient live oak on the banks of the Amite River not far from where the Amite empties into Maurepas.

But Elemore had not worked with the specific thought of a book such as this in mind because, though photography was his pleasure, it was also his business—the way in which he made his living. And so, to a very great extent, his assignments determined his coverage. Obviously he would cover southern and southeastern Louisiana (his own section of the state) the most thoroughly. His work for the Louisiana Forestry Commission and the Louisiana Forestry Association frequently took him into western and northwestern and north-central Louisiana. But his own interests, his own keen eye, dictated much of what we see in his work. He was, we see, and perhaps because he had grown up on a farm (the son of a country doctor), more attracted to the country than to the city; he liked all people, but it was the plain people who interested him most as a photographer: the menders of nets, the fishermen and the farm hands and the moss pickers.

If Elemore Morgan's coverage of his state was of necessity sporadic, it was probably more extensive than that of any photographer before him. It is a guess—but a safe guess, I think—that he had at one time or another, on assignment or on his own, visited all of the state's sixty-four parishes. But in making the final selections for this book we have not thought in terms of specific towns or cities or parishes. A photograph which another writer might have captioned "Rice field near Crowley," I have seen simply as "The Prairies" (the listing of photographs at the end of the book is somewhat more specific). In choosing this approach, in attempting a fairly broad and, I hope, reasonably balanced coverage, we have had to discard a great many excellent photographs which otherwise might have been included. For example, Elemore's photographs of the antebellum houses of the state would make a small book by themselves (and did: *The Sixties Ended It*). Yet in a book entitled *The Face of Louisiana* we could find room for only a relative handful of them. Likewise, some of the photographs included for reasons of balance and coverage might not have found their way into a book with a narrower focus. We have, however, tried to subject the photographs to the criterion both of content and of photographic quality.

Obviously, in a book such as this, the text is there to provide glue, to point the way, to suggest possibilities. If I have not said what Elemore Morgan would have said (and, of course, I have not), I hope that what he felt and what I feel about some of his photographs are not too much at variance. Occasionally, as I went back to his collection, I came across a bit of evidence in this regard that was happily reassuring. For instance, in the very beginning I saw the photograph on page 35 (one of my favorites) as "Every Man a King." Later, as I wrestled with the text with the picture in front of me, one word hung in my mind: *vagabond*. Elemore Morgan, years before, had pencilled in the notation "The Utmost Freedom."

In the last years of his life Elemore and I worked together on a book which I have already mentioned—his photographic study of a tree. I say *we* worked; it was Elemore who did the work. I was to do the text, and to help him make the final selections. And so, over those two years he would make yet another trip down to his tree on the river south of Head of Island; bring back more photographs; print some; discard some. The book on the tree was never published because it was never finished and because all that Elemore Morgan saw in that tree, his wonderful vision of things, died with him. His son and I have, however, brought a small selection of those photographs into this book. One is at the top of page 7. Another is on page 24. And there are three at or near the end of the book (pages 150, 152, and 162–63).

The Face of Louisiana is Elemore Morgan's book. But it is also, in a very real sense, Elemore Morgan, Jr.'s book. The help he gave was invaluable. His close association with his father, his familiarity with his father's work and with the prints in his collection, his own talents as an artist—these were some of the assets he brought to the project. He worked beside me every step of the way in the process of selection, and he worked alone many days in his father's darkroom making prints to replace the original prints which had been damaged over the years or which for one reason or another were not available. When the job of culling proof-prints and prints seemed bigger than either of us had imagined, Dorothy Morgan, Elemore's widow, spurred us on with words of encouragement.

Dick Wentworth, Bob Nance, and Jim Crain all gave their enthusiastic support to the project and helped in ways too numerous to mention. I would especially like to acknowledge the fine job done by Barney McKee in laying out the book and in handling the hundred and one small details which have to be taken care of before a book is finally sent off to the printer. I would also like to acknowledge the help given us by Edith Atkinson of the Louisiana State Library staff, Louisiana Art Commission director Jay Broussard, and photographer Dave Gleason. All three were friends of Elemore Morgan and had worked with him, and the suggestions they gave were extremely valuable. Several of the prints reproduced in this book are to be found only in the collections of the State Library, and Mrs. Atkinson graciously made them available.

CHARLES EAST

THE FACE OF LOUISIANA

When you have watched the sunsets on Vermilion Bay and the sun rise
on Black Lake; when you have hunted hogs with Hanse Coon in the
hog country; when you have seen oil spew from the ground or the
bottom of the Gulf; when you have gone to a place called The End
of the World, and then gone beyond; when you have visited among
the fishermen and the moss pickers; when you have photographed
the gulls and the men who steer the ships and the ruins of Belle
Grove and the main street of Ville Platte and a country church in the
Felicianas and a cathedral in New Orleans . . . when you have done all
of these things you will know how varied Louisiana is. You will also
know how difficult it is to catch the face of it.

It is pine hills . . .

And prairies . . .

6

And woodlands and marshes.

It is stillness . . .

And motion: ducks flying north, or south,
depending on the season . . . rushing waters . . .

*It is alleys of oaks and the houses
at the end of them . . .*

Barges, shady streets, the blaze of oil refineries . . .

And it is people . . .

Most of all it is people.

What was it like before we came? Were the swamps as silent as now?

And what of the rivers? Did the rivers
run down to the sea, dark with silt, still
cold from the ice of melting glaciers?

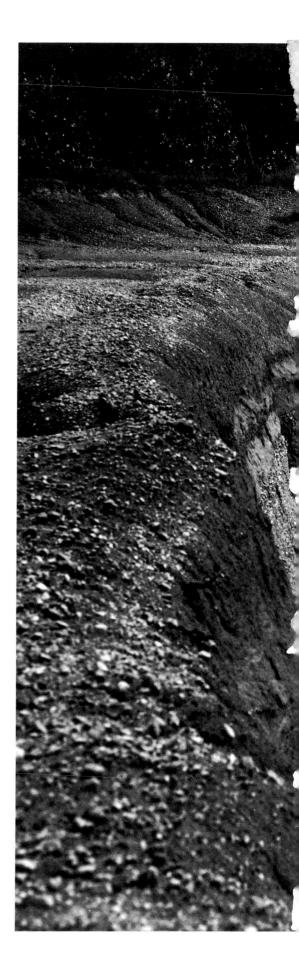

What do we know of the past? Our own past?

What are our monuments?

DEDICATED TO
THE MEMORY OF
OUR SOLDIERS
OF THE
CONFEDERATE
STATES ARMY
1861 —— 1865

TELEPHONE

What is our history?

*It is written here, too. Read it in our faces—
in the face of this woman . . .*

In the face of this man. We are the children of exiles and vagabonds, explorers, adventurers.

Our faces are theirs: the Spanish, the Germans, the French . . .

And those people of legend, the Acadians . . .

*And the Anglo-Saxons. They came later, most of
them, by flatboat and wagon, out of Virginia
and the Carolinas . . .*

And the Negroes, who came in bondage from the Indies and from Africa and who were sold like cattle on the slave blocks of New Orleans.

*And those who came earliest of all, who came
so long ago that we can only date their coming
by the relics in their mounds. They are gone now,
except for a handful . . .*

*But our towns and rivers bear their names: Tickfaw,
Atchafalaya, Tchefuncta, and the river the Indians
called Old Big Strong, also Father of Waters.
Mississippi. Were we to name it now, might not
the name be River of Destiny?*

There is no other like it. But there is the Red, a mighty river too, flowing down from the plains to its junction with the Mississippi.

*And there are the bayous—the Boeuf and the Teche,
Bayou Lafourche, and some whose names are known
only to the moss pickers and the fishermen.*

*And the lakes and bays. At sunrise and sunset
they are at their loveliest; the light grows
or fades. The water catches it all: light and
shadow, sun, sky, cypresses . . .*

Our landscape can be stark, but it is also beautiful. Cane fields run to the horizon . . .

Trees grow tall . . .

The ground over which the hunters ride curves with the winter's plowing.

We are a part of this land.

We live on it . . .

Make our living off of it . . .

We were baptized in its waters.

We are young, old, rich, poor, proud, vain, determined. We are all of these . . .

We who mend nets . . .

Bring oil out of the ground . . .

Fell the trees . . .

Steer the ships through the river's passes . . .

70

Farmers, oystermen, welders . . .

Look at us. Look at all we have built or planted or in some way left our mark upon and you will know how wasteful and capricious we are—but also how gifted.

We cleared the forests, plowed the fields . . .

Tamed the rivers . . .

We built the towns we live in . . .

And the cities . . .

And we dreamed. How we dreamed!

Their very names enchant us: Belle Grove, Bon Sejour,
Belle Helene. But paint flakes, plaster crumbles . . .

And perhaps the columns were never as tall, or as white, as they seem now to some of us in memory.

The architecture of our age is simpler, plainer:
dog-trot, shotgun, VA-FHA, plantation modern.

*Home, of course, is where the heart is. Home is
a sleeping dog, a porch to sit on . . .*

A window to watch from . . .

Home is a shady yard . . .

And a woman tending her geraniums.

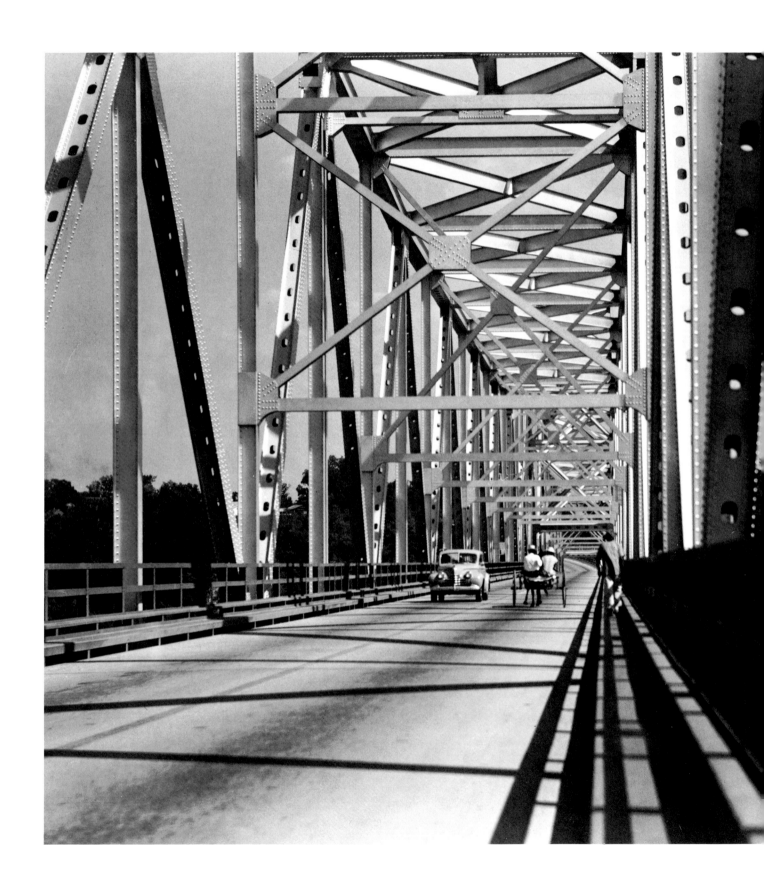

We are a curious blend of the old and the new . . .

Of innovation and tradition.

*We bless the cane, that the crop will be a good one,
and we bless the shrimp fleet on the eve of its
departure: may the catches be bountiful . . .*

But the old ways are changing. Once our cotton was picked by hand and our cane was cut by hand.

*Now the pickers and the harvesters are gone;
the houses stand abandoned.*

We are still a farm state . . .

We plant and harvest more than our share
of the world's rice . . .

We grow tobacco and sweet potatoes and hot peppers, and in the spring our highways are lined with the vendors of strawberries.

But the farm state is going industrial.

The pine trees that we grow will supply gum
for turpentine and pulpwood for the mills
that make our paper.

*We have learned to treat our forests
as our riches . . .*

*But these are not our only riches. We gather
moss from the trees . . .*

And fish from the waters . . .

And from the ground we get oil and natural gas . . .

And salt—and from above the salt domes, sulphur.

*It was oil that made us rich, changed our landscape,
our way of life, brought the tankers and the barges.
Oil for the engines of the world, and the byproducts
of oil—gasoline and chemicals.*

The pace of things has quickened. But there is still time for fun . . .

Time for the simple joy of holding a pole in our hands, or riding out on horseback with the dogs at our heels . . .

146

And there is time for meditation . . .

And reflection.

This, then, is our face . . .

But even now our face is changing . . .

Day by day . . .

Hour by hour if we could measure it, one season to the next, as years fall away . . .

Now solemn . . . now gay . . .

One thing we can be sure of: we will not look quite the same . . .

When we have come to the end of the century.

THE PHOTOGRAPHS

The date given is the date the photograph was taken, as nearly as can be determined. In most cases the source of the date, as well as of the identification, was the envelope in which Elemore Morgan filed the negative. It has not, however, been possible to identify all of the photographs—that is, to name all of the people or to give the specific places. The asterisk indicates that the print reproduced in this book was made by Elemore Morgan, Jr., from a negative in his father's collection. In all other cases the print used was the photographer's. Where there are two photographs on a single page, the order of the listing is from top of the page to bottom.

THE PHOTOGRAPHS

THE PHOTOGRAPHS

THE PHOTOGRAPHS